Red Clay Gypsy

Red Clay Gypsy

Poems

Maria Ingram Braucht

Press 53
Winston-Salem

Press 53, LLC
PO Box 30314
Winston-Salem, NC 27130

First Edition

Copyright © 2015 by Maria Ingram Braucht

All rights reserved, including the right of reproduction in whole or in part in any form except in the case of brief quotations embodied in critical articles or reviews. For permission, contact publisher at editor@Press53.com, or at the address above.

Cover design by Kevin Morgan Watson

Printed on acid-free paper
ISBN 978-1-941209-26-4

In memory of my beloved husband, Bruce,
who left a note saying,
"Wherever your life takes you,
don't forget your Southern roots."

Contents

Prelude
What I Want out of Life: 1976   xi
What I Have Gotten out of Life: 2015   xiii

I. The Early Years

Me, Brought to You by Quaker Oats	3
Shepherd Hill Spring	5
Black Kodak: 1938	6
Family Reunion	7
Miss Minnie	9
Backwoods	11
Home Is a Verb	12
Melanie and the Summer Peaches	14
Moment God	15
The Deception of Spring	16
Myrtle Beach	17
Stars	19
Tobacco Harlot	21
Baudacious Baptism	23
Aunt Ola of Abbeville, South Carolina	24
From the Journal of My Mother Marie	25
One Story beneath the Pin Oak	27
Into the Deep	28
Straw Noon	29
Selling Chinquapins	30
Summer Captives	32
October Confederacy	33
The Keeper	34
Song of Miss Morgain Lawford Sung on the Tailgate of a Mill Hand's Truck	35

The Enlightened Burning	36
Standing On Higher Ground	38
Eventide	40
Across the Road	41
Grand-Daddy Dillon Praises His Mules	43
Just Their Way	45

II. Travels

Twilight in Bali	49
The Season of Mangoes	50
Alexandrian Sunset	51
Egyptian Bird Market	52
Desert Girl	53
One God	55
Flower of New Orleans	56
Outside Karditsa	57
The Obligatory Rite	58
A Feast for the Eyes	59
An Alexandrian Requiem	60
Connemara Morning	61
Caribbean Prize	62
A Greater Beauty	64
Stepping onto Santorini	65
Silver Horn	66
The Homing of the Doves	68
Lasting Out the Storm	69
The Women's Car	72
Caribbean Sugar Bird	73
A Thing Called Light	74
A Greek Spirit	75

III. Back Home

The Waiting Room	79
The Celestial Flag	80
Sweet Emma of the Preservation Hall Jazz Band	81
A Scarlet Trio	82
The Void	83
Opal	84
April Bird's Visit	86
Stop.	87
The Treasure Unearthed	88
Song of the Free	90
The Rose of Shepherd Hill	91
The Wanderer	92
Taking Flight	93
The Shore of Home	94
Author biography	97

What I Want out of Life: 1976

I want a liquid tapestry of
darkness and light and spices.
I want to walk on Italian tiles
barefoot among albino peacocks
and own an emerald that burns
greener than the color can reach,
have canaries with names of prophets,
Bessie Smith music,
lots of shellfish to eat
and ice, violets, gardenias,
bouganvilleas, little sleek brown cigars,
lemons and cream, real gold earrings,
dreams to keep me thin,
and a baby I can dress up like a wedding cake.

What I Have Gotten out of Life: 2015

There's this rustic Egyptian emerald on my finger,
five golden bangles on my wrist, and
a pair of precious gold lotus blossoms I wear in my ears.
They display who I've longed to be.

I have snuffed out the little brown cigar.

I never had a canary
imprisoned from the skies it longed for.

I've had plenty of shellfish, ice, violets, gardenias,
lemons, Bessie Smith music and what not.

The only baby I bore was from another's womb.
The mother graciously shared those little
fingers that would wrap around mine in a loving clasp.

The gypsy in me has wandered in peril,
most times in bliss, but she has come back
to a world of familiar sparrows and finches.
Peacocks, ostriches, parrots, and toucans
have taken nest in some nostalgic far-away.

And I have come to rest in the hallowed,
sweet sanctuary of my red clay home.

I.

THE EARLY YEARS

Me, Brought to You by Quaker Oats

In the noon
dogs licked puddles of
rainbow water by the gas pumps.

A big orange Gulf sign,
my sun banged in the wind.
If flowers burned somewhere
under a different ball
I knew nothing of it.

I could not tell you how many
frolics made up a summer,
but I knew well how many bananas
it took to make a pound.

I learned my multiplication table
lying on the shelf between
the BC powders and the Red Devil Lye,
coached by farmers whose
tobacco juice danced
the Mexican Hat on the stove—
"Aught t'ms anything's always aught."

Mary Janes in my cheeks,
El Producto rings on my fingers,
my job was to draw kerosene
and turn the calendar each month
to yet another RC-crazy hussie
in a swim suit.
Lips the color of oxblood shoe polish,
hair the curls of Toni:
sinful things, Mr. Singer who
came once a week with hair in
his ears claimed.

He boasted two sinful things he'd never done
were drink a Coca-Cola and kiss a woman,
and I wondered how he'd got
Luther and Sudie Bess Singer into this world
without kissing.

I fell in love with the Merita Bread man.
I hid behind a pyramid of
Wolf's Head Motor Oil every time
his truck turned in.
My heart beat hard and I took Tums.
It took two Playtex mountains
beneath my T-shirt to get me to rise
like a sphinx
and witness a hard shame put me down.

I wondered about many many things
but there were few answers.
If your snuff's too strong it's wrong.
A bay leaf will keep weevils out
of your Aunt Jemima.

I grew old.
I must have died.
I learned answers and got me a new sun
that didn't bang and I'm told it's better.
I do know darkness is darker.

Shepherd Hill Spring

Down at Shepherd Hill
we rode the pickup
with cardboard boxes
for the new dirt.
Her apron dancing
off her lap
to April's ragtime,
my mother was happy.
Rich dirt, she pronounced it,
for her flowers,
and swept it up in her hands
and had me smell:
incense of clean rain,
fresh ferns, new lizard eggs.
Going home
with the boxes spilling,
we taxied the old crate like
a chariot, high, high,
lashing at the pistons with
our switches turned whips.

Black Kodak: 1938

In this yellow picture
my father had a monogram K for Kernersville
sweater on he never got to graduate in and
stood grinning by a burnt chimney with
the house all gone.

In that exposure
what portent evading even
the negative held to light
hovered?

What spirit had him wearing a Panama
in the tobacco rows
or slinging scythes,
welding metal to metal,
the firefalls of sparks from
his only wand
dying on the concrete

Or allowing for his thirst
a half gourd of water

So that he wandered the earth
through a geography book
and listened to his life
through His Master's Voice.

Smelling of electrical shorts,
of hay and sweet-cured tobacco,
he held me in another way
than he held a gourd,
explaining galaxies he
wanted to know,
the sisters and dogs
of the cold night sky.

Family Reunion

Daughter of cousin Rubin
after Theodore, who was
Aunt Addie's eldest farthest removed
by way of Pink, who was really
Pinkney Dwiggins of Hardware,
specializing in Number 9 nails and
wart removal by lantern light,
picks alto.

Inlaw Claire, who married Jess and
Miss Maggie's third who
went to the West Virginia coal mines
never to be spied again
wants soprano, and begs a show of
sister soprano hands which fly up
on arms the size of chicken necks
all over the room.

Void, who marched to the courthouse
soon as she could read and changed
herself to Boyd, tam-headed youngest of
Peora's, having caught every warm egg pitched
to her from a hayloft,
tucks her dress to the back of her knees
and remembers shape notes.

Brothers Glenn and Virgil
let out the bass that hides in their throats.

They sing about sheaves
somebody is rejoicing bringing in.
They sing burning bush joy loud
about a roll that's going to be
called up yonder on page hundred fifty-nine

when all the Dwigginses, fat on milk and honey,
gonna holler "HERE!" present and accounted for
with country ham baskets and chow chow for the Lord.

They know the young won't carry on.
Already they don't know half these people.
They gather together each year to
eat sweet potato pie and
sing soprano loud and
say goodbye.

Miss Minnie

In our home place, the porch wrapped around
the front of the house like an apron
with a wide, hanging swing where
my brother and I could watch
Miss Minnie walking to town.

She was always looking back over her
shoulder in startled suspicion of
what might, at any moment, pounce upon her.

Miss Minnie was dark as a star-barren sky,
nervous, and prickly as a briar.
We giggled, without her knowing it, and
shouted, "Hey, Miss Minnie!"

She'd dart into the ditch, as if we were
the very Apocolypse, and come back to
her senses and say a tiny guarded "Hey,"
which we only imagined we could hear.

Miss Minnie would then commence
walking, flinching, jerking around at the
slightest ladybug landing on a weed.

We never wondered about the events in
her life that might have led her to act
like such a scaredy cat.

When she crossed out of earshot,
we cackled like crows.
We ran in to tell Mama we'd seen
Miss Minnie walking into town.

"Let her be, young-uns," Mama chided.
"She's got some thorns in her side
even Doctor Whitaker can't pull out."

My brother and I eventually stopped laughing
and came to wonder . . .
But we never stopped shouting
"Hey, Miss Minnie," as she was passing by.

Backwoods

I've not been here
when you weren't somewhere
watching,
pretending you weren't.

What you get out of
seeing me
lace this spring
with bluets
and cool my feet
is something
I'll never figure.

I think I'll hitch
my dress a little;
the sun's so warm.

Home Is a Verb

Only crossbred birds and Southern girls home.

I cannot look at Cairo's dovecotes for long
without conjuring those devilish red
chickens complaining about the yard,
legs hesitating like the feet didn't want
to set down in something hens had done,
descanting judgments with no pity in them.

Each time I return and sleep and wake
I find notes, little rag-proofs of who I am:

Winter 1968   Here's a sausage cooked.
              You can have it and
              Make you a sandwich.
              Turn light off & heat down to 65.

Summer 1970   Go out back door.
              Front one won't close
              Good and Wind
              Blows it open.
              Get you some okra.

Winter 1971   Put that raincap
              On your head.
              Turn light off & heat down to 65.

Summer 1975   Here is a gardenia.
              Pick you some more flowers
              To take home with you and
              Tomatoes because they just go bad.

If I ride the strange golden waves
as prow-paramour, heaving deep and rising

like a star against the spray,
it is only for the going and the coming back

For I am a tidal daughter
at a helm steered by the fragilest moon.
I am a daughter eating sausage in a
rain cap, having no use for one.

I have brought no branches;
they have waved no palms.
Nor is it for harbor I home.

Melanie and the Summer Peaches

Bad storms in August is why
I perch here on this stool and
swat flies while my mama cans peaches.
I do not belong here.
I know the alphabet of the owl
when he comes from nowhere into
the night to hoot his name.

I know what a fish mouths when he
surfaces,
feel in my skin the darkling rising
of its going down.

I watch my mama move among the pans,
playing their drums to a roof-rain music
she cannot get the rhythm of, else
she would unlock the screen door for me,
say "Shoo, bad little storm, fly to
that high pitched whistle I reckon you hear."

She pours into jars an amber thick as
voodoo, dark with cinnamon.
Knowing she can save peaches by
releasing them to magics,
what business does she think I have
swatting flies, and does it
occur to her the
why of flies,
the ripe they're after?

Moment God

I met an old woman with spots on her hands.
"Life ain't cheatin' you on nothin', is it, child?"

"No'm."
I was barefoot in April's mud.

The Deception of Spring

In that little wooden church
I knew that Christ would come
find me, turn me across his knee and
paddle me big time for my sins
which were a plenty.

Women waved cardboard fans from
something like ice cream sticks
sporting a picture of what they thought
Jesus looked like, kneeling against a
rock at Gethsemene.

The fans advertised Davis Funeral Home,
suggesting that every last one of us would
die and need their coffins, white satin pillows
and their injections of chemicals that
would make us look like who we were not.

I never believed any of it.
I thought my mama's lap would forever
cradle my drowsy head and that bees
would buzz, lilacs would bloom, and
a sparrow would warble the signal of
an ever recurring Spring.

Little did I know God's handiwork,
how an April frost can
kill blossoms door-nail dead
on a budding tree.

Myrtle Beach

Our family was beach-bound through a
five-hour drive every summer,
snaking the back roads of the Carolinas
until the trees began weeping gray
tangles of Spanish moss.

I pretended to sleep on the back
floorboard of the car while my
brother Jimmy stretched out on the seat.
Oh I loved that floorboard where I could
hear the engine singing our way.

We'd stop to split a watermelon under
a tree somewhere and swat tiger-striped bees.

One summer, we took our Grandma Addie
and her friend, Miss Plumy Hester.
First time either of them had seen the beach.
And first time Jimmy and I had to sit upright
and behave, watching the Burma Shave billboards
coasting by, counting cows.

Grandma Addie had stitched herself a
bathing costume on her Singer sewing machine,
pedal to metal, mid-calf, blooming like
a morning glory.
But she hadn't told Miss Plumy.

Once we got there, Grandma Addie put on
her thing and waded into the waters at the edge,
mesmerized by their comings and goings,
some God-driven clock of wonders
baptizing her spirit anew.

Miss Plumy stood on the shore among
sandpiper footprints, looking forlorn—
until she fished out some safety pins from
her pocketbook and pinned her billowing
dress into pants.

She waded out, joining the rhythm of
the sucking, sighing surf, and let out
a squeal she'd forgotten she had.

There they were, two old women,
laughing like wind chimes at the edge of
a sea that reached to shores they could not imagine.

Stars

My father showed them to me
while the arithmetic tears
dried in moons beneath my eyes.

I could not know the sums
and divisions that played from his hand,
but marching across the end of
his finger

There were Orion,
Carina, the magic harp of Lyra,
laced bracelet bells
against the black.

And they hung with dark
answers even this man
cradling me couldn't get,

Almost swallowed in the
inverted Dalmatian night,
fogged with lucidity,
these stones

So pale and far
sometimes you had to
look beside them
to see them.

When I fell asleep
he carried me in
across his shoulder
and I pretended
I did not wake.

Tobacco Harlot

The summer cicadas are rattling in
the trees, aching, it seems,
pulsing the hot tympanic music of
August, when nothing else stirs.

They surge and die,
just like everything else in this world.

Leaves abandon their stems and
float down, copper harbingers of
the requiem to come.

The earth is weary from labor pains,
just as we all were in that summer of 1949,
when I stood by the palate of dried tobacco leaves
awaiting the incoherent babble of auctioneers.

I was stationed there on duty,
meant to show how adorable I was
and how I needed new saddle oxfords for
school, and how the golden leaves we had stacked
were fit for the finest Marlboros.

Clean face. Check. Bright smile. Check.
Hair braided into two pigtails. Check.
Raggedy shoes. Check.
Dirty fingernails. Check.

But wait—should I show that smile?
It might mean I am happy as a tree-frolicking monkey
and don't need no tobacco money.
Maybe I should look sad, like those
orphans on TV raising pledges.

We settled upon a solemn look.
The world was not lost exactly;
neither was it found.
A conclusion was left to be drawn.

And then they came, the huddle of men,
in the same surge as the cicadas,
yelping, babbling, burbling, bidding,
taking not so much as a glance at me.

And then they were gone
just like everything else in this world.

Baudacious Baptism

I guess I was about eight, that summer
the preacher took us all down one Sunday to
Blues Creek for some baptisms.
We weren't even Baptists.
We were Methodists, accustomed to little
sprinklings of water over our heads at the altar.
This dunking business wasn't our thing.

Beulah Barrow was the first and last to
be lowered into the muddy waters of
tadpoles and frogs doing the long-armed
chest stroke, like bloated spiders.

She clinched her nose and back she went,
cradled in the arms of Preacher Pollock who
shouted New Testament words along with
too many of his own.

"Lord, receive this woman,
Beulah Hairston Barrow, into the
kingdom of your grace.
Into the land she was named after.
Wash from her the dark sins that
hunker down in her soul and
shine your light into her washed-out,
clean chambers. Amen."

Beulah's skirt ballooned above the waters
like a jelly fish and her feet started kicking.
She might drown now, I thought, and
Bailey Bledsoe's hound started howling from
the bank, sensing trouble.

By her own strength, Beulah emerged,
coughing, spitting, gasping, cursing,
wobbling about on her legs to stand.
"You son of a bitch, that was too long!"

I hid behind my mama's skirt.

My voice wanted to come out and rally
the congregation into protest.
I wanted to shout "Preacher, this ain't right!
You near 'bout drowned Miss Beulah!"
But I was cradled in cotton and silence.

Every dish on the laid out picnic table was
snatched up in tin foil and every un-reborn
Methodist scattered like pigeons home
with their deviled eggs.

I eventually emerged from behind my
mama's skirt to stand upright and say things.
But I have forever cowered behind something,
fearing not the Lord's mysterious ways,
but those of his fervent followers.

Aunt Ola of Abbeville, South Carolina

Aunt Ola, old, sweet prize,
every five minutes stepped on her
porch to look through cataracts for
our car loaded with nieces of
her dead husband John,
careening from five hours of
driving through mud holes in
backyards, off-course.

She gave us stories,
overhead light,
four beds of hand-stitched quilts,
damson jelly and talcum powder,
a sack of pecans she stooped to
pick from her spitting tree;
anything she could find,
she gave.

We drove off, leaving her by
the camellia bush, waving,
waving,
until she was a heat beam
shimmering in the rear-view mirror.
We knew we would never see her again.

She had said "I love your bones."

She must have taken the bothersome
shade from the lightbulb she kept
banging into
and sat for a time,
hearing one ungiveable pecan after
another drop on her tin roof,
and at night, the gunshot
when the trees bloom with wind.

From the Journal of My Mother Marie

Bad-blooded and exiled,
the Indian just after
night snuffed out the sun
sauntered by the house on
a mule to feed a note into
the winesap and to go on to
wherever it was he made out he went.

My mother,
before she was mine,
would sail across the yard
to fetch the pulp
with its cidery sins
branding her hands—
My swethart Marie—

Her father would suspect,
What business has that boy
with whiskey for blood
on this road every night?
My mother would examine
the scab on her elbow,
wishing dark angels
to cleanse her.

The Indian would hit
yellow jackets one spring
on his tractor at
a bad place in the field.
They were to rise up like
an anthem and leave him
the only good Indian
in the buttery nuggets of clay.

Bees bees bees
my mother would keen into
sighing trees
to make sure no one was listening.

I hear her say bees
when there are no pines
to sweep the word away.

But he was sorry as gully dirt, she says.
I didn't love him so much as
I ached for a dream I could not tag.
There were always games of
snap and tap and tag and,
truth be known,
I was pretty good.

One Story beneath the Pin Oak

Sunday afternoon we're sitting in the
backyard spitting seeds out of
bought watermelons and my father says
it's the worst summer since 1930, when
they had to replant tobacco four times,
on into July, before it took hold.

Six and a half acres brought
a hundred and forty-two dollars
at six cents a pound.
But there were some, he said,
only brought a half, a quarter-cent a pound.

One old man from Stokes County
crated up a bunch of chickens to
bring with him.
The auctioneer's fee was more than
his tobacco brought,
so he took his chicken money to
get back out into sunlight.

They sat around the camp,
laughing to keep from not laughing at
the fine mess they were in.
Young'uns needed saddle oxfords and
notebook paper.

Daddy asked the man from Stokes
was he going to raise tobacco next year.
"Oh yeh," he said. "That's the only thing
they's any money in."

Into the Deep

We let the well bucket fall from
the rope of a worn oak spindle,
down, down, until we could hear it splash.
Like a shore fisherman, my brother
tightened the slack, teasing our prey.

The bucket filled and sank with
cold earth water divined years ago
by a man with sling-shot shaped twigs
from a mulberry tree.

I reached for more than water.
Hanging over the edge of the well,
I whispered down words my brother couldn't hear.
"Come live in me."
"Live in me and take me away."
It was the dark unknown I thirsted for.

Gypsy spirits dwelled in the deep.
They danced down there with chiming
bracelets, strumming on harps,
banging on tambourines,
blowing honied breaths into golden pipes,
and riding on rainbowed zephyrs.

When we cranked the bucket up,
there was, to the frail human eye,
nothing but water.

But I know better.
Spirits answered my call.
I've been wandering for years.

Straw Noon

You fields come to my waist again
lifting and bowing colors of old guitars.
I've watched thirty of you go by,
some neck high,
some bosom for the shortest time.
Your secrets broken with my questions,
we meet predicable now.

You audible earth
loop the beginning of your end to
the end of my beginning—
a noon woman where no shadow is,
behaving myself,
boring myself.

All the amulets I've hung aren't
worth their garlic and
I bore me,
I bore bore bore me
with my bracelets and
comfortable longings.

Knit me with your weeds
and willows and reeds
into your becoming dusk.
I fear I might, like one more
slug in the harrow,
drag my body where my life has been.

Selling Chinquapins

In the Blue Ridge Mountains
around a curve with parking spaces
Mama has a stand of sourwood honey,
blackstrap molasses and a few
striped watermelons.

She has spelled out their names on
a plywood sign for the wheezing cars
that round the hairpin to maybe pull
over and see.

Summer is bad business.
Radiators boil over and people are mean.
They show us nothing but license plate
because they just want to get to a
LOOKOUT and see.

I will never know what it is they think to see,
for there is not a thing in these
mountains but more mountains.

But when the leaves turn sour and fall,
we young'uns play a trick.
We stand at the hairpin with a sign
and hold high in mason jars what
we've scoured the early morning
bushes for.
We holler "CHINK-EE-PINS!"

Because none of them know what
a chink-ee-pin is, they pull over
and we pour a pint of the little brown

nuts into a spread of paper and
twist it around.
There's forty-five cents in the bandana.

Then, because they're in low gear,
they pull into the stand where
Mama is handy with her wares.

Leaf-turn is good business.
Come night-fall, we spread out on
the oilcloth covered kitchen table
what happened.
Mama fries apples and sings
"Fare thee well, Old Joe Clark"
tapping her shoes on the linoleum floor.

Leaf-turn is when my mama laughs again.
It all has to do with those shiny brown
chink-ee-pins and her smart,
conniving daughters.

Summer Captives

We would snare Junebugs
with twine and fly them like
struggling kites through
the buoyant summer skies.

We would catch fireflies
in a jar as winking lanterns
to light our way.

And we would take a twig
and burrow down into doodlebug
powdery mounds,
twisting, teasing, chanting
"Doodlebug, Doodlebug,
fly away home.
Your house is on fire and
your children are all gone."

They'd wiggle up into the
sorrow of daylight, stunned.

Cruel children,
our toys were the innocent
fruits of earth.

October Confederacy

for Jim

Birds got to the persimmons
before we did.

Headed home through the cornstalks
we felled the brittle spires
like Goliaths,
pudding-hungry and silent.

There'd be times
we were to remember it.
You were half my army.

At the back steps
we picked beggar's lice
off your kickers
and my corduroy britches.

Together like that,
how were we to mind Lute Purvis,
pudding on his tongue,
laughing at us through the dahlias.

The Keeper

I was a hider by nature
until Nell was paid
one dollar a day
by my mill-working mama
to keep me.

Keep me keep me keep—
bolts and locks
and bars and stocks
chains and fetters
and wax-sealed letters.
Why,
no one could keep me.

When it was July,
I'd hide in the high grasses;
I'd hide in the firewood box
when it was cold.

Nell did not let me
hide anywhere when
it was anything.

She flushed me from
every sanctuary with
her big black dog and
his Indian scout nose.

That I grew accustomed to sunlight
was a bending of my ways
and I screeched bat-like about
the yard, lost in the found place,
dying on the air,
longing for that sweet cradling cavern
I almost see in mirrors now
when I close my eyes.

Song of Miss Morgain Lawford Sung on the Tailgate of a Mill Hand's Truck

I think I been too long
ironing
for seventy-five cent a hot hour.
I think I been too long
thinking
when is a train coming in.
I think I been too long
living
without having a good time
to myself.
I think I sit right here
'til somebody come steal me,
do what they will,
me busting with hosannas
in my heart.

The Enlightened Burning

Alton Barrow's barn burnt down.
Sparks could be seen for miles
across the dim Autumn sky.

Everybody bundled into pickups and
brought sweet potato pies and
new-fangled Jell-o recipes with nuts and
fluffy marshmallows.
But it didn't do any good.
It didn't make a mark upon his sorrow.

He hunched over, smaller than the
bantam man he was, and kicked cinders,
smoldering little nests of fallen fire, said,
"God has not been good to me.
He has smitten me with his awesome handiwork
which I do not appreciate."

The Methodist women said,
"For shame, Alton. Don't go blaming God for such.
Now taste this Strawberry Dazzle, it's called."

But Alton didn't taste anything but bitter bile.
He drew the curtains across his windows
and coiled in the dim, broken life of shuffling
shoes across hardwood floors.

When Winter cloaked its crystal blanket over
the timbers, some educated woman from the
community came to visit, without any marshmallows.
She said, "Alton, there's this Chinese proverb that
says, 'Now that my barn has burned to the ground,
I can see the moon.'"

Alton sat for a moment in silence.
Then: "Them Chinese people is smart.
It's the holy Lord's truth.
The moon was always up there,
but it was always in the middle.
I never knowed it to rise."

Standing On Higher Ground

If we stayed rocking
in the yard chairs
long enough after supper
we'd hear Happy Knob Church
come rejoicing.

We could finish our stories
while the pickups popped
the gravel they'd taken up
collection to lay.

We could give up looking
for company through the first
ten minutes of prayer.

But when the preacher must have
shaken his handkerchief out,
we hushed.

Mama wouldn't let us laugh
but it was not disrespectful to grin,
which every last one of us did,
for the squeals that jubileed and
the stomps than thundered
wouldn't let us study Jesus solemn, like
we did at the Methodists.

It was like hounds triumphant through
the woods on a scent sweeter than corn bread.

Once I witnessed them take
somebody possessed of the Holy Spirit
down to Blues Creek and
push him under by the head until

he liked to have drowned and
his overalls ruint because it was
red catfish mud and not a bit like Jordan.

Mama commented they were smart to
put their money into gravel and not
a piano because you couldn't have heard it,
and we were allowed to laugh too loud for
what she'd said.

But somebody in that church had a tambourine.
It would rattle like a hailstorm come to
judgement on our roof.

In bed being cold I would have my
knees against my chest with my
fingers cupping my toes.

I would be almost warm before
I heard the owls dare their
Old Testament gloom.

Happy Knob was to bust open
Gates of Heaven with a tongue for a key,
a shout for a crown.
Any meek Lord would just stand there
with a lamb in his arms
and let them rush in, taking over sweet
meadows with their tambourines.
I knew they would all make it.

And I feared for the Methodists.
For though we were poor,
we were not poor enough to
thank Jesus *that* much.

Eventide

Sweet merciless time is
cawing like crow against
a darkening sky.

Some ancient zephyr scatters
leaves into whirlpools that rise,
fall, and die.

I've never let go of Spring.

Long have I reveled in beginnings,
nurturing dormant eggs until
they gave the fearful crack.

Then I would fly away, Oh Glory,
like a hummingbird, looking for
the perfumed snare of
something else to come—
lilac, honeysuckle, the coiled
promising bud of a rose.

The somber silence of Autumn
stole upon me like a thief.

I did not have the good sense
God gave me to see the sun going down.

Across the Road

Every July we'd pick, string, and hang in
the rafters of a barn the ripe leaves of tobacco.
On a break, we'd delve into the sweet
wedges of a watermelon.

Tony, a man of dark descent, always got choked.
We'd slap him on his back until he
coughed up a crimson blob and breathed again.

His brother, Tip, was a drunkard,
tipsy day and night as a moonshined-up
hound dog with a howl.

Tony tended to ignore him, to let him
simmer in his own thieving poison.

One Sunday, Mama and I visited Tony,
rocking on the front porch and nibbling
his sister's fatback-smeared sweet potato pie.

Tip, who lived across the road,
dipped his face into water and then
into a pan of white flour.
He wobbled up to us in stumbles,
tripping on things that were not there.

"You gonna talk to me now, Tony?
Tell me you gonna talk to me now."

Tony examined his own fingers and
said softly, "I wanna fry you like one of
our mama's pancakes in a skillet of
syrup born from stinging bees."

Tip said, "What'd you SAY, white man? I couldn't hear you.
I'm gonna have to rob a raccoon of his ears
and perch them on my head like a Mickey Mouse."

"While you're at it," Tony whispered to
his fingers, "steal the brain from a donkey
which is way yonder bigger'n yourn."

Granddaddy Dillon Praises His Mules: Kate and Jane

They did everything I bid them do.

Mules is smart, I can tell you.
They will up and jump a bob wire fence
if you throw a blanket over it.

And they have patience, will abide
most tribulation, will not be foundered.
They know when to stop eating, as
straight-bred horses, cows, and donkeys do not.
I've found myself in the midnight punchering
gas out of a stupid beast's stomach and
keeping watch by lantern light.
Too much clover, too little brain.

Not so, the mule.
He is naturally smart as a whip.

And he is hard to come by.
He won't produce his own kind.
The chromiosomes is all wrong.
You have to take a horny male donkey
and let him have a go at
a female whore horse if the moon is right.

Once you've got one, he can out-plow
anything, even a tractor, and rest just as easy
as if angels coiled in his ears.

Kate and Jane let my corn grow tall as
it wanted to, without messing with it,
and they tilled my potatoes so gentle
not a one was sliced through.
Them potatoes was laid up like terrapins

on a creek bank for the gathering,
smooth and slick.

And I miss them.
Jane ran off smarting from some buckshot
from a confused hunter on October,
and Kate died, I reckon, from a lonely heart.

Just Their Way

Every Saturday, my grand-daddy,
Atlas David Dillon, known as "Ack,"
would take a chicken from the coop,
trap its wings with his hand into a
betrayal of embrace, and
whack its head off on a tree stump
with a sharpened axe.

Oh, the desperate floundering of the
body, twitching like it had been
attacked by a swarm of bees,
until it grew quiet, resolved,
and dead.

Come Sunday, Grandma Addie would
merrily cook its parts, dredged in flour,
fried in lard rendered from slaughtered pigs.

I curled on the kitchen bed,
sucking my thumb against a hard
pillow stuffed with hard feathers from
some deceased. No sissy thread count.

I was too young to know why
I was never hungry.

And they were too backwoods bred
and needy to realize any wrong.

II.

Travels

Twilight in Bali

I count three, four, ten, then only
Krishna knows how many geckos are
scampering across the walls of my
low-fare motel in this Hindu land.

Maybe they just swallow flies
like Miss Piggy's friend.
No malevolence.

But these tails flick back and forth,
a silent metronome
suggesting some wickedness is seething—
some startling pounce to come.

Across the Ayung River,
the Maharaj has placed his palms on
his knees and is chanting melodious
vowels which still my soul.

I bask in a serenity without fear.
I cross my arms against my chest
and close my eyes.
I dissolve into this tranquil world.
What is—I let be.

Come daybreak, the walls are bare.

The Season of Mangoes

The season of mangoes is short and vivid
like a lightning-crackling glimpse of brilliance
in a midnight, starless sky.

You cannot eat a mango politely.
The juice streams down your arms in
a passion not to be constrained.

"Love me!" the mango teases.
And I do, sweet exotic you!

I plunge into your depths,
all watery and voluptuous,
into your very marrow until
I come to a mossy, unyielding stone.

As much as I seduce you,
I cannot get to your heart.
You will not give.

Alexandrian Sunset

The splendid hour of the
golden-orange mosaic of sun has come.
It strikes earth's anvil like a copper coin,
barely audible,
streaking a metallic luster
across a trembling sea.

It is going down by the heartbeat,
slipping westward
by the breath, never to
come again, not precisely,
not in this exact glorious gown.

The same sun that lolled so
lazily in the noonday sky
is melting down so fast.

Birds home. Pigeons circle
the last light and come flapping
down to the aviary, signaled by
a lone man waving a flag on
the rooftop, to remind them
where home is.

And there is the smell of
curling wood smoke, and the voice of
the muezzin, rising like a plume and
falling just enough to be caught and
brought up again like Turkish taffy.

It is a wondrous wail,
bringing the day home to roost.
There is this fading,
precious light, and
the painful knowledge of
its brevity.

Darkness is imminent.

Egyptian Bird Market

Amidst the din of the souk
prism-colored birds twitter, squawk,
and cry the cry of a lonesome wind.

Pigeons sold will be stuffed with
cracked wheat and roasted until their
skins appear shellacked.

Vibrant birds meant to fly will
end up in cages on stair landings
as burdens to be fed.
Their sorrowful chirps will go unheeded,
misconstrued as song.

There is a girl-child with a common
chicken tucked beneath her arm,
wandering through the sun-zebraed aviary.
She wears a white scarf already,
hibernating into Islam.

She touches the beaks of birds and
strokes their webbed feet, whispering
amethyst words only spirits can comprehend.

A love-wanderer.
She is maybe six years old.
Her chicken is not for sale.

Her wandering will last until she, herself,
may be fettered in serpentine vines,
and her own benevolent heart is caged.

Desert Girl

I am sitting on a rock in the Sahara,
waiting for the radiator to hiss the
steam free and die down enough to
accept more water down its throat.

It is so quiet I can hear beetles
scampering, flicking little puffs of dust.
I can see lizards darting about in
brown, electric flashes.

Then she comes to me.
From out of nowhere, she comes dancing,
anklets jingling, kicking sand,
to touch my hand and blink hungry
earthen eyes at me.
A brazen, dusty brown child.
A jinn, perhaps.
What is it she wants from me?

She touches her lips, then her ears,
and shakes her head "No."
She cannot hear nor speak, a common
malady among the Bedouin, from,
they say, either inbreeding or the
incessant hot wind.

I make a pantomime of reaching into
my pocket and handing her something.
She shakes her head "No."
What, then?

I am too American to understand.
In the sonorous silence,
she lays her hand upon mine and

just stands there, smiling.
She wants nothing more from me but that.

She brings to me the gift of the
dazzling water of her eyes,
so chestnut brown they look silk,
and they quench my thirst.
My own engine has died down enough to
accept the grace of this little spirit that
jingles across the sands.

Maybe there is, in the hereafter,
a whitening of the dark, the land
we hold in promise, that
beautiful hymn book shore.

But there is great treasure here,
buried in the earth,
awaiting excavation.

The language spoken is that of
her dusty little hand upon mine.
I will never know her name,
nor from whence she came.

All I will remember is that
she brought water to my dry,
parched soul, and flitted away
like a butterfly.

One God

In Istanbul,
my room was the size of
a closet, space enough to
walk in and lie down.

The first muezzin, the Muslim
call to prayer I ever heard,
rippled at the breaking of dawn
just outside my window.

The lonesome cawing
of crows joined in.

I perched my knees on
the mattress and leaned out
into the nocturnal skies slowly
becoming light,
listening to a lifting and plummeting
of a quivering voice
that, in my hungry soul,
re-affirmed there was God.

Not A god,
but God.
The only One who can be
a merciful companion
in my wayward journeys
and bring me home.

Flower of New Orleans

Hey, Brooks Brothers' suit,
Gucci boot,
ten-speed lover with
the juicy fruit,

Tearing through the quarter
like a bat out of Savannah,
flashing yo' manhood in a
Manhattan manner...

I mean there ain't no dire need
for nothing.

But if you feel like company,
if you feel some slow, sweet song
rising in yo' throat like a night jasmine
just turning open,
COME.

I will give you Coca Cola to drink,
and rum,
and crawdaddies to eat,
and we can watch the horticulture
creep through the window like serpents

And I will read to you
Tennessee Williams' recipe for key lime pie,
which don't talk about condensed milk.

Ain't nothing good condensed.

Outside Karditsa

The old man claims he can
mount the mountain in five minutes
with his seventy-five-year-old legs.
It is true.

His wife squats on the kitchen floor
to pluck feathers from a chicken.
He is racing up the mountain,
she is plucking feathers,
and night, with dark talons,
lights upon the earth.

The percolating bells of sheep
round the hill, white now
by a cloud of clouds on foot.
The shepherd stops at the gate
to say how fine the fig trees
look this year and how
the olives will be bearing soon.

We build a fire with lemon wood,
cook the chicken, dish up
the yogurt, wash the scallions,
pour the wine.

What Argo,
what ship is this that carries us
through the incubating dark as family?
What hand pours the oil of music
upon my head and
makes me call this old land home?

The Obligatory Rite

Whether for the first or
fortieth time
from the Acropolis
look over bleached, sad Athens
to the flowering corpses of war,
poppies the crimson of blood.
Shoulder the brooding sun like
a cross, stoop to loosen
your sandal in flesh as
Attika's Nike did in stone
and feel the thirst,
the quick of the insatiable
heart that rises on colt legs
to stumble for new pastures
and the pastel fans of mimosas,
the glacial pain of water.

It is the kindest mercy that
we do not die but that
we are born a thousand times.

A Feast for the Eyes

    Alexandria, Egypt

Little Noor sat with her Baba on the street curb,
eating ful wi' falafel. Beans with those little fried
balls of chickpeas.

Their donkey cart was parked in front of them,
bearing baskets of picked oranges and purple,
papery blossoms of the Bougainvillea—hoping
to sell them to passersby.

They dipped torn ears of bread—Aish Baladi—
into the creamy, cumin-scented beans.

Their hungry eyes darted like flitting hummingbirds
from the beans, to the donkey, and to each other.

Theirs was a grateful, sunlit world,
softer than any cashmere, gloriously
confined. No one else could enter it.
Not all the kings of Persia.

An Alexandrian Requiem

She dreams on the balcony
in the city of musk and memories.
All the Europeans have fled
to homelands;
all the bars have shut down,
and all the marble stairways
have been nubbed at the edges
by thousands of haunting footsteps.

The sea water crashes
against the corniche,
spraying the passing cars
in a salty rain.
Windshield wipers flap back
and forth like a metronome
measuring the sweet cadences
of Brahms.

Sunlight is splintered by
feuding, darkening clouds.

She leans over the railing and
lowers a basket by
its rope to the street, where
the vendor exchanges the
one pound note for six lemons
and gives her a grateful nod.

She brings it up,
winding the rope hand by hand
in the accelerating wind.
The basket becomes another
swaying rhythm of a mournful song.

The skies are electric.
Day has taken on the sinister cloak of night.
There is a storm coming on.

Connemara Morning

for Jennifer

Sun breaks through the round
keening of the wind,
cold and gauzed with winter mist.

Waking
with this tiny life beside me,
this little fledgling,
watching the sleep fall
from her eyes, I dawn.

Ours is a nest of
Molly Bloom flannel,
a landslide of goose coats,
and the smell of rashers
sizzling downstairs
under the Catholic's hand.

We are too new to speak.
We stir,
we blink at the window
where the wind rounds its mouth
with cold gray vowels
and at each other we blink
and at the virgin
holding a bauble of a heart
where her heart should be
and we stir.
We blink.

Those white horses
that ride the sea
are breaking and breaking again,
watery heartbeats,

they will ride out the moon
as long as there is moon.

And we are here
in a brevity
we have neither the light to deny
nor the darkness to know.

Caribbean Prize

I have come so far to see this blue.
I have sold the fine cosmetics of
Mary Kay with such frenzy,
I have been awarded this particular
blue of a spectacular sea.

I can sit here in my straw hat and
order Pina Coladas until the
darkness steals in with birds
seeking roost.

Well, I seek roost too.
I seek it every day of my life.
I have minimized my own wrinkles
(straw hats help), and have mastered
the technique of what we call
juvenescence.
That's French, I think.

But there's blue,
and then there's blue.
They are never the same.
Sometimes it's the bird chirping
with promise.
Then there's the sadness of being blue.

It takes a discerning eye to
sort it out.
Mine is very attuned.

For instance,
I can tell you that that handsome
boy folding the umbrellas will never,
in light-years, ask me to dance.

A Greater Beauty

At the edge of the lowland sea
where the waters ripple with
whispering wind,
a white swan is held inexplicably captive.

His leg is tied by a cord to
a metal post.
Maybe it is an attempt to
cruelly imprison beauty,
to hold it there in twilight.

The mate is free to swim
away as she wishes.
But she hangs around,
waddling the blue waters in
allegiant grace.

He is hers and she is his.
She is just as captive.

Stepping onto Santorini

I did not know how I would be
changed by a vista.
I could have turned from the
path behind Petros and his donkey
and gone home intact.

But the donkey had my suitcase,
and Petros was tapping him down
the lozenges of steps and steps like
a hiccup. And so I followed.

How was I to know that love
travels so well? Old love,
lost love, every love I ever felt
glowed like tiny votives in
the temple heart.

So that when I stepped upon the
precipice, with the entire Aegean
hundreds of feet below and
thousands of miles an aching blue wide,
my knees buckled.
I had to sit.

I can tell you of an absolute stillness.
I can tell you a donkey brayed from
some far away, and a bee buzzed.
One single bee worried a clump of thyme.

That is all I can tell you, except
I knew then the treasure of my life.

Petros looked back from the stones
below, quizzing me.

You funny old man, gold-toothed
sage with sun-buttered face,
and a wealth of spirit behind your own eyes,
do you not see that I am tired of going?
Do you not see the honied breath of
lost love breathing upon me,
and how I carry it now to this
ancient place where olives grow
from barren earth?

In this sacred solitude, I realize that
nothing that has whispered its song
into my heart is ever lost.

Know me.
I am here on this step,
listening to the song of a bee.

This is exactly where I am.
I have, after life-long labyrinths,
come.

Silver Horn

She came home this time
with amaranth garland and fragrant
rosemary for remembrance tied
in a gauze pouch with string.

When she closed the door behind her,
the workers' song went back into the
hills and died with the earth.

No, the man standing by the fire had a beard.
It was not Carbonne who was always clean-shaven
and played a silver clarinet.
But to be sure, "Carbonne?"
He stood bent over, warming his hands
and, glancing sideways, knew she was there.

"Carbonne!"
She danced with laughter around the room
with flowers in her hair and sang :
> "Oh I have come from kingdoms far
> To fetch the world before thee here…"

But he had changed.
His eyes made the fire grow dim,
and hers, punishing the almost, drew free.

"Two summers ago," she said quietly,
"With the silver horn."

The silence was deafening.

She lay the amaranth garland in the fire
and, drawing the rosemary close to her breast,
was gone.

The Homing of the Doves

At sunset,
when the voice of the muezzin is quivering
through the Alexandrian skies,
the doves circle in a choreographic splendor.

They will eventually come to roost
where the man on the rooftop waves his flag.

"Come home, come home . . . all who are weary,
come home."
A Methodist hymn enters my mind in
this Islamic terrain, instilling a camaraderie.

The doves have strayed, billowing in
God's reckoning, across a beaming sun,
to claim their own will.
They have flown into the unknown
and sipped the intoxicating nectar.

In the end, they will come home,
meek and comforted, forgiven,
settling for the sweet roost
they have always known.

Lasting Out the Storm

It is all gold, somehow,
the night where shadows flicker
across the walls from dozens
of honey-colored votives.

I've built myself a shrine to
last out the storm here at the
jumping off place of the Aegean—
Oia, on the tip of Santorini.

I have provisions enough.
A bowl of red Easter eggs, some anchovies,
capers, potatoes, a chunk of cheese.
I have a bottle of raki, because I read
about it in Lawrence Durrell, how
old men would drink it beneath plane trees
and slap down backgammon.
I could taste it in the pages.

And I have Caruso himself, scratchy,
wailing from two biscuit-sized speakers.

Molten, this room takes on ambers and
embers and I will burn the night long
like some topaz scorching the earth.

Horizontal rain pelts the window in
a hungry cadence, wanting inside,
wanting to blow my house down,
snuff my gold.

Then there's a whining at the door,
a pawing.
Yellow dog, little more than a puppy,

wet and shivering, comes into
our house, Caruso's and mine.

He gets a frisking with a towel,
and sparks his tongue.
This yellow dog loves olive oil and
Easter eggs on a floor plate.

"For the main course, Monsieur Dog,
may I suggest an Easter egg cut into
moons with a sliver of anchovy and
the slightest whisper of dill?
And don't you just LOVE Caruso?"

Belly-full Yellow Dog favors the folded
square of extra blanket at the foot
of my bed. He places
symmetrical paws by the sweetest
face of closed eyelids.

Outside, metal posts are being plucked
from the concrete like flowers.

The wind is a symphony around the eaves :
tenors, basso profundos, and a
melodious siren mourning all
the lost boys at sea.

She is in black, this wind,
covered from head to toe to
swarming, rippling, Greek widowing black.

We are the only ones, it seems,
in gold.

Me and Yellow Dog, the haunting candles,
and Caruso.
And we are a mere 14-carat.
Nothing too precious or brittle.
Oh, we will last.

The Women's Car

The sand from the Sahara, given the ride of wind,
occasionally blows across Alexandria and
clouds up all clarity.

The squeal of the shuddering tram on its narrow veins
pierces the dust-tormented afternoon.

Daisies wobble along the tracks in a
deep-rooted persistence.
Their white petals are not plucked by the
wind; they do not fly away.
They are grounded with a yellow face which
is staunch, even in the fog.

I am sitting in the women's car, segregated
from men, where scarved young girls are
absorbed in pocket Qu'rans.

Older women stare bleakly out the windows,
contemplating the fate of such
deeply rooted daisies.

Sometimes they glance at me and smile.
My hair flirts blatantly with the wind.

We are sisters on a short journey only
our eyes can comprehend.

The tram rumbles on to the station—
screeching to a halt at Mohated Ramleh,
where we scatter like briefly
acquainted birds lifting into flight.

Caribbean Sugar Bird

She call me Sugar Bird, my mama,
'cause I always flying over sand and
it get stuck on me like
I some sweet cake dusted.

She sell she bracelets she make
on de beach of Bequi, our home.

When de sun set gold on de water,
go we home and wash she me
from the sand, peek hard with
unbelieving on my face like
she done just found me.

Say she, "Sugar Bird, where I be
without you?"

A Thing Called Light

On the tarmac in Jakarta,
awaiting my brief flight to Bali,
I stand alone among strangers.

It is midnight and the skies are
electric with dry-heat lightning,
silent veins of splintering white.

A lust has shepherded me to this land where
women balance towers of fruit on their heads
and burn incense to fragrance hungry
multi-armed deities.

I will ride the back of a dapple-skinned
elephant into a wilderness of ferns and
brazen monkeys scampering in devilment,
in thievery of the slightest shiny thing where
moss cloaks every stone.

A lone man, his legs scissored beneath him,
will chant for hours,
the echo of his voice will ripple across
river waters up through rice fields into
an orange imploding dawn.

All this, I don't know yet.
I stand on the tarmac, where fear crackles
through my veins just like the lightning
crackles through the sky.

My yoke will be lifted by
this thing called light.
It will illuminate my way.

A Greek Spirit

I am called Zorbaiki by
the villagers because I am a little
Zorba and I dance my way
through everything.
No need for bouzoukias strumming.
I dance to my own rhythm.

They all tell me, "*Katse kala,
Zorbaiki,*" which means sit well,
behave.

When I see something?
Like a fish jumping out of
the water and catching the
wet sunlight like he is
wearing diamonds, I whoop!
I cry with joy in my heart.
I am seeing him for the first time.
Ever.

People cast their reins out
to calm me down.
They say, "*Katse kala,
Zorbaiki,* get used to it;
that is the way of a fish."

Oh, I hope I don't ever
get used to it.

III.

BACK HOME

The Waiting Room

Melina had spent her life
with it tucked beneath her arm
like a coveted treasure,
waiting for some signal
to set it free to roam the paths
of peril into ecstasy.

If life were a tree,
she had hugged tightly to the trunk,
never climbing up
nor venturing out on the limb
to capture the fruit that would be
surprisingly there.

Now the thievery of time has
brought age upon her.

She sits by the fireplace alone,
watching cinders being sucked up
into fireworks through the top of the chimney,
flying into some unplanned choreography
of radiance in an unimagined sky.

For no reason she can think of,
she cries, like she'd done when
she was a little girl in that department store
when her balloon was bobbing on the ceiling
and nobody could reach that far.

The Celestial Flag

Far away,
through the dark
entrails of night,
your light flickers like
fireflies in my soul.

You signal my way
through solitude and exile
into a dawn of yearnings.

Without you, it's all
an echo of what has been.

Sweet Emma of the Preservation Hall Jazz Band

I have worked like a plow mule all my life.
There is some sweet Canaan, all I know.
Golden bayou, chili pepper sauce.
I'll be among that number
sure as I beat hell out of these piano keys—
Luden's cough drops on the tenor,
pocketbook in my lap,
gonna lay my burdens down, let 'em be.

It won't be for the shirts I've starched
nor for the floors I've scoured,
they don't amount.
They'll just say up there SWEET EMMA—
They'll have the make 'em step back a'ways,
let me pass.

They'll be wantin' me to sing, and I'll sing.
They won't say it's pretty, Lord, they know
it's not pretty.
And they'll be apt to say, "Give that woman
a catfish for her tribulations; let her be."

And I'll just traipse in my petticoat,
knowing my real talent lies in these fingers.
If I know Jesus and his daddy—
and like middle C I do—
they will arrange to have a piano.

A Scarlet Trio

I don't know what came over me.
One minute I'm living life proper-like,
with my hands crossed in my lap.
And then some wildness erupted that
felt OH so GOOD.
I danced to a rhythm I didn't know I had.
It maybe had to do with that moon thing.
But whatever, I'm KEEPING it.

It was just hot, you know, with the
sun blazing down and all that cold rum and
steel drums knocking out that slam beat.
I just got s - w - e - p - t away like
white sand on a waning tide, and, well,
I WAS rather more jubilant than was called for.

I didn't mean anything by it.
I just went with the music.
Next thing I know I'm Delilah on
a tabletop, dollars growing from
me like leaves on a willow—
which is how I came to
re-evaluate my day job.

The Void

It's the shuddering silence that
brings on hurt. It even echoes.

A bird sometimes sings.
There's a scampering of a nervous squirrel.
A raccoon stands up on hind legs
with sexy black eyes and asks
something I do not understand.
I say "Shoo!" He reluctantly goes.

None of these companions will ever
give me the music of your voice,
the velvet of your touch,
the sweet lilt of your laughter,
nor all the harmonic chords that
once ran through my veins
like a symphony.

Opal

Opal is older than
she makes out like.
She's real little too.
When she walks to the store
all you can see is umbrella.
You think where is that
umbrella going?
Opal hangs it between
herself and a world grown
too large for her,
a dull, blue bubble bobbing
down Fourth Street.

Her children are gone from her,
to California, and she
doesn't like to have them back.
"They're so grand now," she says.
"They make me squirm.
Whatever I do is not the way
it is best done.
They eat bee pollen and such like.
I don't get it."

Opal's house, like the new world,
is too big.
She uses a cotton placemat for
a backdoor rug and confesses
she might altogether disappear from
this earth if allowed to stay.

"One thing is," she says, "if I make it
to Higher Ground, I'm going to announce
right off that I don't want one of

those mansions as advertised.
I want a little cottage I can
keep clean and a plot of black dirt
where I can set out day lilies."

Her lilies are another thing.
She digs them up by the armload and
gives them away to anybody,
foretelling the extraordinary crimsons,
ochres, the majestic magentas, the
bruised burgundies they will bloom to be.
They are always yellow.
But nobody tells Opal.

Behind her curtains at night,
she unclasps a box and
hangs old jewelry around her wrists
and neck and tiny little ankles,
adorning herself in splendors past.

She searches for something small and
meaningful in the box, something she can
lift to the light and recall
how large her life was lived.

April Bird's Visit

An inquisitive little bird—
I'm not Audubon enough to know its name,
but smart enough to know the dull feathers are
those of a female and not the flamboyant flirts of
some fly-away male
perches on the windowsill with
some scrap in her beak,
peering at me,
searching for a sign.

Maybe she is seeking a signal,
some "go ahead" to begin construction of
the nest she already builds.

Somewhere inside the hollows of my
heart, I realize I never carried a twig,
never built a nest,
never hatched an egg.

I stare back at her with momentary envy.
But there's a distinct camaraderie.
I wave to her and wink my
"DO it, girl!" approval.

She cocks her head, gives a peck on the window
without releasing the straw, and flies away to
whatever she was doing before she met me.

Stop.

Now the V's of geese glide
southerly, with that bead of time and
direction sewn into their plumage.

The yard is noisy.
Like wading through old parchment.
Colors are brilliant, but sour,
smelling old and lost and lonely.

I know the world is full of rhythmic
pulses, dancing to a music we cannot
hear, except through the silence of a
meditative heart.

Oh I long for just one more
afternoon when the world would
stop its going, when it would freeze,
like a thieving photograph steals from its prey.

You would be there with me and
I could reach out and touch you.
Like that—the camera would click us still.

The Treasure Unearthed

for Bruce

Oh, my love,
we kicked our heels high into
a benevolent sky that made us know
that together we could fly about like
hummingbirds seeking nectar.

Your wing, with a deliberate touch,
gave lift to mine.

Nectar we found, which fed our
spirits with some honied
elixir which dizzied our minds.

And fly we did,
bumping into clouds,
surviving thunderous wrongs,
and as rods, the lightning we
attracted buzzed our love into
a glorious frenzy.

And then you left.
Your body went away.
Your smile, your touch, those
bluer than azure eyes,
your laughter dissolved into
puffy ashes that now fertilize
the garden we had planted.

You were gone too soon.

Manure makes a flower thrive.
We gave it plenty of that.
We also gave it fountains of water and
a merciful God poured sunshine
on its head.

The garden blooms now with weakened
blossoms that knew a better day.

I could not miss you more.

I know you have gone to that other
beautiful shore where waves lap
my arms around where you are.

And I know you wait for me, with
maybe a bouquet of those fragrant
gardenias we, against all odds, and
in the catacombs of our hearts, grew.

Song of the Free

In the pew of an African-American church,
I heard the re-birth of a song I knew by heart.
The woman pulled, with the seductive fingers of
her voice, the pulsating body of heart and heat and
hunger from the congregation.

"It was—it was—it was—it was
GA-RAAAAACE that brought me safe thus far,
and I know it's gonna be that same,
that same,—don't you know it's gonna be that very same
ol' GA-RAAACE that will lead me home."

Caught up in the frenzy, I recalled the puny white voices
of my own church, stuck to the notes of some map,
keeping words nailed to them, like on a cross.
Never did they venture down a dusty, dirt road that
wound around in tangled paths.
They started with the first note and ended with the last.

Why were they condemned to be slaves to their music
when the once imprisoned dark ones
rose up in freedom, mastery, and glorious song?

The Rose of Shepherd Hill

It's been said that the sense of hearing is
the last to be lost as death tiptoes in.

My brother Jim and I each held one
of my mama's hands.
Her eyes were closed.
I whispered, "You will always be with us,
and we will always be with you."
Jim whispered, "We love you, Mom."

I want to think she carried our words with her
like a blanket into the dawning light,
climbing the top tiers of the tobacco barn,
strong in shimmering spirit,
dancing body, and fertile mind.

She would often step on my hostas
while helping me with yard work.
When I'd admonish her, she'd say,
"Shoot, you little scaredy cat,
they will come back."

They always did.

And so does she.

The Wanderer

That foreign star
by which I have navigated my way
has been snuffed out.

The light lives on,
but the star is burnt into cinders
which scatters across the night.

I wandered, chasing alluring,
flickering dreams just beyond
my own horizon.

The passion throbbed.
My star shined with the brilliance
of a comet coursing the skies
in a fading, inevitable death.

I glimmered with a frenzied light
in a holy darkness.

But the gypsy has come to nest
in the hallowed sanctuary of home.

Taking Flight

A jet plane rumbles through the sky,
going maybe to lands of palm trees, some
Palmettos lilting like willows in the Caribbean,
others erect as paint brushes, dangling clusters
of unreachable medjool dates in the Middle East.

I sit on my garden bench,
bound to where I am.
Birds chirp in the trees singing
staccatoed songs of what seems
like contentment.

Some scamper across the grass in
a cadence of 1-2-3 . . . sometimes 1-2-3-4 . . .
and if I make a sudden sound,
1-2-3-4-5 FLY AWAY!

All of them have wings.
They can fly anywhere they want
without taking off shoes and placing
them on a conveyor belt, or raising
their wings to be patted down and searched.

The world is theirs for the taking.
Yet they linger here.
I long to see what their open,
non-blinking gratified eyes can see.

The Shore of Home

Whether we have danced by the Aegean
to the strums of Zorba-inspired bouzoukias,
rollicked to the tympanic clinking of cymbals,
meditated to a Hindu chant across
a rippling river,
or been lifted in spirit by
an a capella South African choir,
we all live in the shadow of mortality,
and we will, eventually, all come home.

Maria Ingram Braucht was born in Kernersville, North Carolina, and attended Baylor University, University of North Carolina at Chapel Hill, and the University of Florida before receiving a B.A. in English Literature and Drama from Pfeiffer College. Her poems have appeared in various magazines and journals, including *Carolina Quarterly*, *North Carolina Poetry*, *The Beloit Poetry Journal*, *The Oconee Review*, *St. Andrews Review*, and *Malahat Review*. Her debut book of poems, *Maria*, was published by Red Clay Books in Charlotte, North Carolina, in 1976, followed by her selection as one of five poets for inclusion in the anthology *Thirtieth Year to Heaven: New American Poets*, published by Jackpine Press at Wake Forest University in 1980. She operated an international specialty foods and coffee roasting shop in Winston-Salem, North Carolina, called Maria's, for 33 years, from 1972 to 2005. During that time, her passion for traveling and experiencing different cultures was fulfilled.

www.ingramcontent.com/pod-product-compliance
Lightning Source LLC
LaVergne TN
LVHW041341080426
835512LV00006B/554